Mind Spill

Miriam Noyes

Presentation by *BookLeaf Publishing*

Web: www.bookleafpub.com

E-mail: info@bookleafpub.com

ISBN: 9789363307810

First edition 2024

DEDICATION

I dedicate this work to my Self.

For all the tears, the years, the betrayals, the bruises, the cigarettes, the binge eating and alcohol benders:

They did not break you Noyes. You are still here. Telling your story with the Word, with photography and dance. We are here!

Ahmen

ACKNOWLEDGEMENT

I would like to thank Freedom House, Volunteers of America, Verizon and the National Multiple Sclerosis Society.
Freedom House and Volunteers of America specifically for saving me at a time when I was in a free fall.
Verizon and the National MS Society for teaching me about the circus of business.

I thank My Self for not giving up and for staying alive.

PREFACE

Since I can remember, I have used writing as a way to manage my emotions. I think most of us have used writing as a therapeutic tool, until we are introduced to the idea that eating and drinking can be a medium for emotional pain; an inviting medium where others can share in our misery to the tune of crunching chips or Taquilla being downed.

The following pieces are about some of life's pains:
domestic violence, relationship recidivism, parental absence due to death, depression and resilience...

So go get your chips and raise your glasses. Welcome to the

Mind Spill.

daddy

I wish you were here. I wish we would have explored your smarts and my diabolical ideas together. We could have ruled these fools, Daddy. We could have been a greater family. I miss you so much that the idea of your not being here is almost maddening...almost. I remember a lot of what you taught me, but I execute those lessons with a sour grapes attitude finding, I rather be my own company than commit to sharing my peace of mind with another person full time.

I am not understanding why you were ok to reject me at the time of my teen pregnancy. I always wondered how you and Mommy were able to disconnect like that.

I wish you were here.

You would have run this NFT game and actually been able to get along with any one of the men that I dated if you just let go and allowed yourself to be happy and see they were all likened to you. Each with enough of whatever it was that I was attracted to or appreciated more

than the next, was molded after your example.
You and Tim had art and music. You and Ray
had sports and food. You and Chad could have
had a Father Son bond...from guns to ideas about
those guns to art to code to carpentry... he would
have been likened as Your Son.

I miss you, Daddy. I am so sad inside. I miss
Mommy.

I am ashamed of how intensely I miss you both
because I am over 45. I am still in shock by your
absences. I have not recovered from seeing
Mommy's body unalive and empty of the Light
we all treated as her own.

It is another Father's Day weekend, and I am
reminded as I have been since June 2012 how
much I regret not sending the prior year's
Father's Day Card to you. I was so arrogant as to
believe that waiting until next year was better
than sending it late. You would have received it
a few days later, yes, but my sentiment would
have been received and we could have had
another reason to talk.

I am so sorry that I was a foolish and lawless
Daughter. There is still a small space in Me

which does not accept your absence as death.
But simply as an absence.

I dream that the smarts I referred to at the
opening of this letter were used to find a way to
make unalive your legal Self;

and that you are indeed, alive somewhere,
breathing and laughing. Free.

I know you have the discipline to pull off
something like that and that awareness renews
my hope that you are somewhere on this rock.

Alive.

mommy

why

why be here gathered round

weeping and story telling

remembering how and when

eyes sparkling at the thought

Why?

why do all that?

you didn't call to check in check on check up

didn't write to see

nothing

an' now here you all are fkn crying and wishing
around the idea of me

your ideas of Me

the ideal of Me...fk you

sorry assed family I chose

a bunch of gossipers

complaining and lying to the very ones they
claim to love so deeply.

wonder " ..why she waits till almost 50 to talk
about this sht..."

I wonder

out this gentrified high rise windoor

seeing the land and nighttime horizon

the colors

are hopeful shades

the buildings are things on someone else's mind

some days

You just need your Mamma

you need someone who will love you
unconditionally

who will tell you it's alright

 who will remind you it's alright

that you are still loved

questions

cancers of the mind

seduce me

now finding beauty in death

the flowers

the tears

promises of new beginnings

positive talk

can be found in the eulogy of the one we love

but

why now?

more questions

wasting

trivializing the experience

just to be crew with benched believers

those members

counting offerings as if they were blessings

can only offer up

broken staff/s at the time of

the crossing

have you ever been lost?

in a world of familiar

lost to yourself

drowning in recollections of

times past

comfort gone

family gone

new realities

possibilities

forlorn/where is He

to sew up what time has torn in me

or to sincerely

hold my hand

while i mend

grow

the ultimate balance

where?
when?

surprise

I want you in my life.

Because your effect can't be denied.

So why does this relationship have you
surprised?

The space between our eyes holds all of what is
inside.

So surprise

I want you in my life.

seen

All this poetic jive, these phrases, quick turns,
double entendres

plays on words with words about words

All of my imperfections rush to be seen because
they know you're looking when you are really
only
complexly

a version of

ME

You are my test
my confrontation with self

seeing what I would see

were I separated from this flesh

All this poetic jive, these phrases, quick turns, double entendres

plays on words with words about words

All of my imperfections rush to be seen because they know you're looking when you are really, only, complexly

A version of

ME

You are my test, my confrontation with self

and what I would say to me

if I were separated from this flesh

All this poetic jive, these phrases, quick turns,
double entendres

plays on words with words about words

All of my imperfections rush to be seen because
they know you're looking when you are really,
only, complexly

A version of

ME

You are my test, my confrontation with self

and what I would say to me

if I were separated from this flesh

hard vest

My deal is ideal

Free and clear
Free and real

Unheard of passion

My ideal is all powerful

He ties a bow to each of my tears and tells me to
smile

Tells me I am safe

with one hand at my waist, one at my gate, lips
on one mouth to kiss

No sound is heard

My word
my ideal

So quickly can reveal

The fact that I choose to remain free of control

Wanting to know your reasons why

exposes why

you do anything that you do

your reason

And if it means that our season is done?

Harvest

hate is

hate is a real thing

more than an emotion

it creeps up the side of my cheek

seeking teeth and tongue relief

this is where I end and She begins

new thoughts brought on with new walks

hate

is a real thing

11.19.11

The dream of him smothering me. The idea of having to adjust my entire character to be with him was my human selfishness. Because I know love. I know a Daddy. I know a Father.

One who loves doesn't do what he did. How he felt comfortable talking to me less than human. Yet would proudly boast about how he curbed his mouth for money at work.

I know love and surrendered to less.

My baby is here, our baby.

But where is she? What have I welcomed her into?

depression

Across a field of graves is a grave field

loaded with potentials

intending to

meant to

full cycles survived

Depression across time

Chipping parts of me away

my strongest self

but who is holding the ax?

The strongest...

controls the doer

the strongest

is the believer

And should the believer believe
she is worthy of drama

She will receive it

And if she believes she is worthy of love and all
of it's extraordinary examples

then

she

shall

have it

daily reminder

daily affirmations

affirming daily

a daily reminder that
nothing is new

that

that which IS

or becomes

was already knew in silence before becoming
loud

or known to our now

so how do I forgive what I cannot seem to forget

Y am I happier when we are apart

as if missing you is a yet to be explained art

this is your reminder

there is nothing new under the sun

quiet's noise

Today is not what it should be. Trapped inside the shell, silenced by the mouths of the several selves. Just want peace, freedom; quiet's noise. To be able to be quiet out loud without fear, without care for the human eyes, the human ears, so I can be free to BE. Surviving this realm requires focus. And this internal speech must cease because it keeps me bleeding. It keeps me believing that this is real.

bookkeeper

Where did I go?
No.
When did I go?
Was it at the first use of bitch? The first choke?
The first spit?

No, no, it had to be the five yard fridge rack at
my back.
Was it when I allowed talk to talk me back?
Hmm.

No, it had to be that first lie, that first
inexplicable cry at work in the bathroom.
Mirrors the length of six sinks. Should have seen
it, but I couldn't even look at me, couldn't look
myself in the eye. So back I went to numbers
and decimal points, codes and inputs...analyzing
my thoughts with each keystroke, each entry,
letting my debt credit balance sheets be the
cover to the math that I could not figure...

A Love Poem

To open my mind

my heart.

To let it all spill out To watch you sift through it
all To tell you my doubts

To whisper magic with my mouth

To open me up
Have me tender and sweet

To have me, cherish me, kiss me, speak our
understood definition

Breathe me in

cause the quake that changes shapes

makes my nose wider to match my hips

Let's go now and birth this gift we've seemingly
stumbled upon

For we were written

then given

to the air as

each half appeared

knowing the other instantly and forever

No mystery

Lynda Vegas Brown

Sometimes there are times when I am not me

Oh I'll look the same but I'm not me

Sometimes

I don't remember the decisions I've made nor the
acted out plays after I wake

I am not me

I only remembered that I have forgotten
something

Time

important somethings

substantial somethings

I would think that the pain I brought back with
me would have stayed in that moment
that lapse of me

since the white coats told me

that the lapses are due to an overly suppressed
and depressed me

"Miss Noyes, here. Take these and you'll be just
fine. No more losing time and seizing on the
floor in crooked lines. Yes, after these, you'll be
just fine..."

summer aches

some moments I miss him so much I feel out of
sane

like the earth has stopped and I am still spinning

only to remember he is a chemical reaction from
my adrenals

I remember you are a figment of my doing

of MY ruin

neurons firing memories and memes of our last
dance

then I remember you aren't even real unless I
SAY so

so...

my spin

comes to a complete stop and walk straight away

spinning one more time half of the way ..but I
walk

29

with my two feet

Away

From yoU

binge

I say I need a hug

He tells me I'm missing love

I hang up the phone because I am drunk and
didn't call for that sht

I called to have you tell me you missed my sent
on your fingertips

How you miss my lips

Fuck

I am FEELING

I'm feeling open, just like you wanted

So what will you do with me? Talk about love?
That's sober talk

A thin line for the sober to walk.

Not me
not in this condition

not when things are so clear

not missing mommy or daddy or my daughter or
any of the haunts that chase me down every
waking moment

Woods Woulds Wounds

if there was a place I could go

I would

but the woulds have become so popular

they appear as woods

I nap under their canopy

wondering in my dreams

if this feeling will ever let me go

better GO

Don't look back daughter

Stay free

You are better than this

You are better

you are better

you are better and stronger than all of this

Rise

and rise

and rise

and rise

and rise

and rise

and GO!

the Word

Every poem is a person, every person
an experience.

Choose words wisely
Know them
trust them
The Word is our bond
It is what makes US
The Word

Sounds are primers to understanding.

The Word was before the Genesis. Or Jesus. Or
the council that made the Christ. Our very Being
was made
by
with
from

the Word.

Y

You mean in addition to alcoholism and all.that comes with it?

In addition to being cussed out whenever the mood hits?

house items broken?

doors constantly slammed?

In addition to being touched in ways that aren't loving or kind or invited?

In addition?

To talking out of both sides of One's mouth??

In addition to not listening just being quiet until it is time to speak again?

Or

In addition to not listening just talking over me until I am drown out and it's just noise no longer communication?

In addition to blaming others for Your over dramatic responses?

In addition to your inability to see your Self and therefore live as though you are owed?

In addition to your impatience and selfishness? The celebrated cognitive dissonance?

In addition to being so full of One's self that when it's time to focus on ways to face your Self..you make fun of me and delay your own victory?

love

37

When you are loved

You wont wonder

There will be no question

It will Be love

it will be kinship all the way
it will BE love

www.ingramcontent.com/pod-product-compliance
Lightning Source LLC
LaVergne TN
LVHW010916200726
843509LV00013B/1955